For Jaron and Lucy, whose voices of wit and wisdom add
a little more harmony to the world—*BC*

To my parents and brother, who always encouraged and
helped me to find my own voice—*SG*

Books for Kids From the
American Psychological Association

Magination Press is a registered trademark of the American Psychological Association. Order books at maginationpress.org or call 1-800-374-2721.

Book design by Christina Gaugler
Printed by LakeBook Manufacturing, LLC, Melrose Park, IL

Library of Congress Cataloging-in-Publication Data
Names: Cole, Bill (Psychologist), author. | Green, Sarah, illustrator.
Title: Carol Gilligan and the search for voice / by Bill Cole ; illustrated by Sarah
Green.
Description: Washington, DC : Magination Press, 2024. | Includes bibliographical
references. | Summary: "A biography of the life and work of groundbreaking devel-
opmental psychologist Carol Gilligan, who has devoted her life to the discovering,
uncovering, and recovering of voices underrepresented people, as well as recon-
ceptualizing traditionally held views on moral and identity development in young
people"– Provided by publisher.
Identifiers: LCCN 2023046319 (print) | LCCN 2023046320 (ebook) | ISBN
9781433843532 (hardcover) | ISBN 9781433843549 (ebook)
Subjects: LCSH: Gilligan, Carol, 1936–Juvenile literature. | Psychologists–United
States–Biography–Juvenile literature. | Developmental psychology–Juvenile liter-
ature. | Moral development–Juvenile literature.
Classification: LCC BF109.G55 C65 2024 (print) | LCC BF109.G55 (ebook) | DDC
150.19/5092 [B]–dc23/eng/20231218
LC record available at https://lccn.loc.gov/2023046319
LC ebook record available at https://lccn.loc.gov/2023046320Manufactured in the
United States of America

10 9 8 7 6 5 4 3 2 1

CAROL GILLIGAN
and the Search for Voice

By Bill Cole

Illustrated by Sarah Green

Magination Press • Washington, DC
American Psychological Association

CONTENTS

INTRODUCTION

What does the word "voice" mean? When most of us think of that word we probably think of the sounds we make when we speak. But there is also a deeper meaning to the word voice. It has to do with the way we use it when we speak—think of phrases like "having a say" and "speaking your mind." And how we use our voice—or how we don't—makes an enormous difference. The word "voice" can almost be used synonymously with the word "self."

Carol Gilligan is a world-renowned psychologist who has dedicated her life to the questions of how we learn to use our voices, how sometimes we learn not to use them, and how sometimes we learn to use voices that are not truly our own. She has gone on a life-long journey to help discover, uncover, and recover unheard voices. Through decades of research listening to people, she has sought "the story underneath the

 How we use our voice—or how we don't—makes an enormous difference.

story," as she has often said. And what she found has led to an increased understanding of a range of voices in professional fields as diverse as psychology, law, business, nursing, educational leadership, ethics, and gender studies—voices that had been previously ignored. Many transformative moments in our culture since the early 2000s, including the #MeToo movement, heightened awareness of LGBTQ+ rights, Smash the Patriarchy as a viral social media meme, and social-emotional learning initiatives in our schools have roots that can be traced back to ideas Carol has been talking about since the 1970s.

Carol Gilligan came of age on the heels of first-wave feminism, which was the beginning of the modern feminism movement. It started in the mid-1800s and lasted until the mid-1900s, and focused on fights like the right for women to own their own property and to be allowed to vote. The 19th amendment to the US constitution, in 1920, granted voting rights to women and was perhaps the biggest success of first-wave feminism. Susan B. Anthony, Lucy Stone, and Elizabeth Cady Stanton were galvanizing forces in these excruciatingly long and hard-fought efforts.

Second-wave feminism was the women's rights movement that took root between the 1960s and 1980s, led by influential figures like Betty Friedan, Kate Millet, and Gloria Steinem. They focused on issues ranging from workplace equity and fair pay for women, to Title IX laws providing girls and women equal opportunities

"A life history cannot be separated from history itself."

in educational settings, to women's reproductive rights. The movement gradually expanded to be more inclusive and address the needs and concerns of a greater diversity of women, driven by the activism of Angela Davis, Audre Lorde, and Kimberlé Crenshaw. Carol Gilligan's research and ideas would provide key touchstones for many of the priorities of this second-wave movement.

One of Carol's mentors, the famous psychologist Erik Erikson, often stressed that "A life history cannot be separated from history itself." In other words, in order to understand a person, you have to understand the time and place of the world they were living in. Like how a person's work is influenced by their life experiences; nothing happens in a vacuum. This was a driving belief of Carol's as she explored people's voices: how they were used, not used, and even silenced. And it is true of Carol herself, too; when looking at the path of Carol Gilligan's work, you can find a similar path in her life. These parallel paths tell her story and "the story under the story." It is a story of voice.

CHAPTER 1

A Growing Voice

" I remembered the sounds of my mother's voice and the voices of women teachers telling me what I needed to know, their voices often sounding as if they were speaking for someone other than themselves."

Carol Gilligan was born Carol Friedman in New York City on November 28, 1936. Her father was a lawyer and her mother stayed at home to concentrate on raising Carol. She was an only child, and her paternal grandfather lived with the family for most of Carol's childhood. It was a happy home filled with good company and warm affection. Carol was involved in a variety of activities as a child, including dancing, fishing, singing, and playing as the only girl on a boys' softball team. Even as a child, she was pushing boundaries. She went to the Walden School, a progressive school on the Upper West Side of Manhattan that emphasized the visual and performing arts. It was through music, dance, and the other arts that Carol first learned to appreciate the many different ways a person could express themselves. A person's voice was more than just what came from their mouth. Growing up Jewish, Carol attended Hebrew school, where she loved singing in the chorus. Singing gave her an appreciation for voice as a physical thing, too. She was fascinated by the different ways people communicated, with or without words.

Learning to Speak Up

One summer, when Carol was two years old, her mother signed the two of them up for Clara Thompson's institute at Vassar College in upstate New York. It was a progressive program for its time that aimed to give parents training on child development. The children would attend preschool classes while the parents went to separate learning sessions during the day. Set up as a communal experience, at night the parents slept in one building while the children slept in another. Carol remembered loving her teacher and the school part of the day. But she was not quite as fond of the bedtime arrangement. She didn't want some stranger putting her to bed. She wanted her mother. Carol quickly learned about the potential power of voice as she called out in protest for her mother. "I cried so hard and unrelentingly, I turned blue in the face," she would later recall. Carol got her way in the end. The rules were changed and Carol's mother was allowed to tuck her in to bed and sing her to sleep. "She ultimately really valued that refusal in me," Carol later said about her mother. So, Carol learned early on how useful a resistant voice could be. But resistance would not always be easy.

In her early teenage years, Carol's relationship with her mother started shifting. It became more complicated, as so often

> Carol learned early on how useful a resistant voice could be.

happens with parents and their teenage children. As much as she loved her mother, Carol thought she had surrendered a valuable part of herself in order to stay at home and focus on being a mother and a wife while Carol's father built his career. Her mother sent some mixed messages when giving Carol advice, too. Sometimes she would say "Darling, you know! Pay attention to what you know," instilling in Carol a sense of self-confidence and resourcefulness in moments of uncertainty. Other times, her mother would snap at her, "What do you know?! Let me tell you how the world works." This pattern fed a long-running battle within Carol between trusting her inner voice and being tempted to go along with what others said, even when it was something that didn't feel quite right to her.

And when Carol started to get interested in boys, she would sometimes clash with adult women about how a girl "should" behave with the opposite gender. She found herself arguing with her mother even more than before, and one of her female teachers once actually urged her to tone down her "high-spirited" tendencies. Carol was feeling pressure to fit into some mold that she didn't really feel represented the true her. She had an uneasy sensation that a lot of the advice she was getting from these women about how to present herself did not reflect what they really thought. Their voices seemed to be expressing the wishes of someone else. It was as if these women had somehow, somewhere, learned that this was the advice they should be giving young girls about relationships with others—whether the women agreed with it or not. Were the words really their own? Or were they speaking for someone else, like ventriloquists' puppets? And, if the women in this case were the puppets, then who exactly were the ventriloquists?

For young Carol, this confusion led to a sense that there was a divide between the way she was seeing the world and the way the world might be seeing her. This was another early lesson on how the voices we use are not always as they seem—a lesson that would stick with Carol her whole life, fueling her later research on the thoughts and feelings of teenage girls.

Educational Freedom... Social Restrictions

After high school, at the urging of her father, Carol enrolled at Swarthmore College in Pennsylvania. She would consider it one of the best educational experiences of her life. She was in an Honors program there and excelled academically as an English major and a Psychology and History minor. She had a huge amount of academic freedom. There were no grades, and she mostly just had to write open-ended papers on authors she admired, like Virginia Woolf and Leo Tolstoy. She loved her professors. She loved the natural beauty of the campus. She loved the self-paced learning offered by her classes. There was, however, one aspect of campus life that bothered her. Swarthmore, like most colleges in the 1950s, had strict rules about young men and women not going into each other's dorms. People thought it was improper.

Carol was annoyed at the contradiction between how the school handled the academic life versus the social life of the students. Academically, the students were given so much freedom to create their own educational experience, cutting their own paths in how they chose to study. But they were treated like children when it came to socializing with the opposite gender.

DID YOU KNOW?

Many colleges did not even admit women into the same classes as men—or into the colleges at all—until the 1970s. Columbia University didn't become fully co-ed until 1983!

It reminded Carol of the arguments she'd had with adult women over how to act with boys. It seemed like another detached voice of authority attempting to drown out the true voices of the students. This did not sit well with Carol. She spoke out about how unfair she thought this was through involvement on the school's judiciary committee. And she continued to protest in her own way by sneaking meet-ups with her boyfriend in her dorm room. Of course, within a matter of a few years, once the 1960s came along, everything changed. Co-ed dorms were established and men and women were permitted to mix as they pleased. Carol's voice of resistance was often years ahead of the changes she demanded. This pattern would emerge again and again throughout her life.

Carol graduated from Swarthmore in 1958 without a clear plan of what she wanted to do next. One thing she knew she did not want to do was go down the same road as her mother—she wanted to establish a career of her own instead. She applied to a graduate program in England to study Shakespeare, and also applied to psychology programs. Psychology ultimately won out, and she began a doctoral program at Harvard University in clinical psychology. It was still pretty rare for a woman to be in a PhD program at Harvard at the time, but Carol Gilligan was a rare individual.

DID YOU KNOW?

According to an American Psychological Association report, in 1975 only about 30% of all PhDs in psychology in the U.S. were awarded to women. By 2020, 70% of all psychologists in the U.S. were women.

Carol was an avid reader. The books she read and the authors that most moved her played a huge role in the way she came to understand the world. The rich and complicated lives rendered in the works of Jane Austen, Anton Chekov, Virginia Woolf, William Faulkner, and so many others served as vivid and layered representations of the human condition. In contrast, she found in psychology that human beings were too often cast into general categories and described in overly simplistic and flat terms—especially the women..

Carol was frustrated by this. She thought it was

a limiting and superficial way to think about people. It started turning her off to the field of psychology. So many female characters in literature—Jane Eyre, Clarissa Dalloway, Elizabeth Bennett—had these rich and authentic voices, yet in psychology, that individuality was lacking. Where was this kind of depth of character in the psychology books? Where were their voices?

A Growing Family

As Carol was finishing up her doctoral degree, she married Jim Gilligan. They had their first child soon after. Although they began building the trappings of a traditional domestic life, Carol and Jim were also closely connected to the bohemian world of foreign films, folk music, and political activism. Two of Carol's professors in graduate school were Timothy Leary and Richard Alpert. Leary would eventually become an iconic figure in the counterculture and hippie movement, and Alpert would later change his name to Ram Dass and become a notable spiritual guru. Both men were interested in the potentially therapeutic effects of LSD and other psychedelic substances (which were legal at the time), and Carol even got invited to experiment with LSD with them on a beach in Cape Cod. She declined the offer—it didn't seem like the responsible thing to do now that she was married with a baby. Her association with bohemian subculture had its limits!

By 1962, Carol and her young family moved to Cleveland, where Jim was to attend medical school for psychiatry. Carol put her thoughts about a career on hold while Jim completed his program; she spent her days raising their young son and finding other activities she enjoyed. She fell back on her training as a dancer, performing with an interracial modern dance troupe. She also devoted some of her time to voter registration efforts. Carol brought her two-year-old son with her as she walked around the Hough area on the East Side of Cleveland, a predominantly Black neighborhood. She would go house-to-house knocking on doors and talking to the residents about the importance of getting out the vote. She found most people very welcoming, inviting

DID YOU KNOW?

The height of the Civil Rights Movement was from 1954 to 1968. The March on Washington took place August 28, 1963, and the march from Selma to Montgomery took place in March of 1965.

her into their homes to have good conversations about how the act of voting was a proactive and essential form of using one's voice in a democracy. This was especially true for people who were underrepresented in positions of power, like economically disadvantaged people, people of color, and women. Proper representation was a big problem in the early 1960s—and it remains a work in progress to this day.

Carol also had some unfinished business from graduate school. She still had to complete her doctoral dissertation, which was on the outcomes of temptation. Midway through her doctoral program Carol had realized that she wasn't interested in becoming a therapist, as that kind of work would take her away too much from family life, which had led her to shift her emphasis to social psychology. In the research for her dissertation, she had demonstrated that if children were read a story about people who cheated as opposed to a story about people who were honest, the children who were exposed to the story about cheating were more likely to cheat in a game afterward. This suggested that the temptation to cheat could be shaped to a certain extent.

Carol finished her dissertation and earned her PhD in 1964. It was a bittersweet moment. It was undoubtedly a crowning achievement, especially while juggling the responsibilities of being a young wife and mother. However, the general field of psychology was leaving her feeling cold. Between the lifeless descriptions of people in the psychology books, and the icy ways her clinical supervisors had advised her to talk to children, such as "this is not a happy way to be," Carol concluded that this type of work was probably not a good fit for her moving forward. Soon after her dissertation was done, Carol's second child was born, another boy. It appeared she would be leaving the field of psychology behind for good. Or so she thought.

Missing Opportunities

A lot of history is closer than we think!

Try asking a relative, a teacher, or another adult you know about their college experiences. Were there some places they weren't allowed to attend simply because of who they were? Or maybe their parents didn't have the opportunities they wish they had.

What colleges do you know? Do a search to find out when they started admitting women and people of color. Do any of the answers surprise you?

CHAPTER 2

An Ignored Voice

" In Piaget's *Moral Judgement of a Child*, you look up 'girl' and there are four entries. You look up 'boy' and there's nothing, because the child is assumed to be male. Erikson and Freud wrote from an assumed male perspective."

In 1965, Carol and her husband moved to Chicago, where Jim was doing an internship at the University of Chicago as part of his medical training. Jim was friends with one of the deans at the school, who at one point said to Carol, "You have a Harvard PhD. Why don't you teach?"

So she began teaching some psychology classes to bring in extra income for the household. Carol found teaching rewarding, and so when the family eventually moved back to Boston, she kept at it, teaching some psychology classes at Harvard on a part-time basis. It was around that time that, through one of

"You have a Harvard PhD. Why don't you teach?"

her former graduate school professors, Carol met the renowned social psychologist Erik Erikson. Erikson had done groundbreaking work in the area of teenage identity formation, and had developed a famous model of psychosocial stages in a person's life, from infancy to old age.

Carol started teaching classes with Erikson in 1967. She was fascinated by how Erikson used art films in his classes. For example, he showed *Wild Strawberries*, a 1957 film by Swedish filmmaker Ingmar Bergman, which is centered around an elderly and grouchy doctor who is returning to his alma mater to receive an honor for his life's work. During the road trip with his daughter-in-law back to the college, the lead

> "I saw a psychology there that I could join."

character reflects nostalgically on different moments throughout his life—a fitting illustration of many of the ideas Erik Erikson conveyed in his psychosocial life-stage model. Carol was dazzled. She found the use of high art as a way to bring psychological concepts to life immensely appealing. It played right into her deep love of literature, dance, and other forms of artistic expression. She said, "I saw a psychology there that I could join."

This integration of art with psychology when considering the human condition was a revelation, and a potential remedy for the tendency to describe people in ways she found excessively clinical, impersonal, and dry. She was particularly struck by Erikson's key claim that, when considering the human condition, you can't separate a life history from history itself. The person, and the time and place in which the person lived, had to be thought of in relation to one another. This resonated with Carol. It added another layer of depth to the examination of a human life, including her own. Finally, Carol felt she had a signpost in psychology that would point her further into the field. But there were some significant roadblocks waiting for her around the corner.

What is Moral Development?

Carol's reignited interest in psychology soon led her onto the research team of another of Harvard's prominent faculty members, Lawrence Kohlberg. Kohlberg was doing game-changing work in the area of moral development. As one of his research assistants, Carol had a front row seat. Kohlberg was greatly influenced by the work of the Swiss psychologist Jean Piaget, who was best known for his model of cognitive development in children.

Children, according to Piaget, formed an increasingly mature way of understanding and categorizing ideas about the ways the world works as they age. For instance, when they are very young, children tend to use faulty reasoning, such as thinking a nickel is worth more than a dime because it is larger in size, or that the moon is following them during an evening walk when it is actually their perspective that is changing. As children get older, these ideas get refined and more logical. Kohlberg, in turn, suggested that people's moral judgment develops in a similar way, becoming

PIAGET'S MODEL OF COGNITIVE DEVELOPMENT IN CHILDREN

STAGE	AGE RANGE	MILESTONES
Sensorimotor	Birth– 2 years	Coordinating motor responses with sensory information. Understanding that they are separate beings from other people and objects around them. Using language for simple demands. Learning that things continue to exist even when out of sight (object permanence).
Preoperational	2–7 years	Thinking symbolically and imaginatively. Learning to use words and pictures to represent objects. Using language to express basic concepts.
Concrete Operational	7–11 years	Thinking logically about concrete events and concepts. Understanding the concept of conservation, quantity, time, and space.
Formal Operational	11 years and older	Thinking hypothetically, theoretically, and counterfactually. Using abstract reasoning. Applying concepts learned in one situation to another situation.

gradually more advanced as they figure out how and why to act honorably and do what is considered right.

Basically, it was a way to figure out how—and why—people develop the moral compasses that they do. It was a totally new way of thinking about how people make choices. This was a major focus of Kohlberg's work throughout the 1960s and into the early 1970s. In the aftermath of World War II and the atrocities committed by the Nazis in the Holocaust, Kohlberg had moved away from thinking

DID YOU KNOW?

After the Holocaust, many Nazi officials were tried at what are known as the "Nuremburg Trials." There, many of them tried to claim that they were only following orders when they committed atrocities (this argument, the "Superior Orders" argument, is now often just called "the Nuremburg Defense"). The judges rejected this defense, saying it was not enough to excuse them. A person's basic sense of morality was in question.

of right and wrong as flexible matters of purely personal opinion. In light of what had transpired in the concentration camps, Kohlberg believed all of society would be better served by thinking of moral behavior by universal standards: some things were right, and some were wrong.

Around the same time, Carol was involved in the civil rights movement, the anti-war movement, and the anti-nuclear weapons campaigns that were widespread on college campuses in the mid-to-late 1960s. When she had been teaching at the University of Chicago a few years earlier, student grades were starting to be used as a basis to determine who would be drafted for the Vietnam War. Carol protested emphatically. She, along with several of her colleagues, told the

university, "If grades are going to be used to decide who's drafted and who gets exemptions, we're not turning in our grades." The types of moral decisions being made across society were at the forefront of people's minds. Matters of right and wrong were being fiercely debated. Value systems were being reexamined. It was a bit of a juggling act for Carol as she now had three young children at home. But her research—and the implications for society—was important to her, and she figured out how to make it all work.

The Heinz Dilemma

Kohlberg's most common research method was to present people with various hypothetical moral dilemmas or fictional social scenarios and have them say what the characters in the dilemmas should do. The most well-known of these fictional scenarios is known as the Heinz Dilemma.

It goes something like this:

In a far away village, a woman was near death from a very bad disease, a rare kind of cancer. There was one drug the doctor thought might save her. It was a form of radium that a druggist in the same town had recently discovered. The drug was expensive to make, but the druggist was charging ten times what the drug cost him to make. He paid $200 for the radium and charged $2,000 for a small dose of the drug. The sick woman's husband, Heinz, went to everyone he knew to borrow the money, but he only raised about $1,000, which was half of what the drug cost. He told the druggist that his wife was dying and asked him to sell it cheaper or let him pay later. But the druggist said, "No, I discovered the drug and I'm going to make money from it." Heinz got desperate and broke into the man's store to steal the drug for his wife.

Should Heinz have stolen the drug? Was doing so right or wrong, and why?

In the research, the "yes" or "no" answers the participants gave about whether Heinz should have stolen the medicine were less important than the reasons they gave for whether he should have stolen it. The why. There were varying levels of moral reasoning that could be used to justify either stealing it or not stealing it, some more sophisticated than others.

For example, if a reason for stealing the medicine was so Heinz would get the reward of being thought of as "a good guy," that response would be considered lower on the moral judgement scale than a response that said Heinz should steal it because he took a vow when he got married to honor his wife, and stealing it for her benefit would be the honorable thing for a husband to do. From this research, Kohlberg came up with three distinct levels of moral reasoning, from least mature to most mature: the Preconventional Level, the Conventional Level, and the Postconventional Level.

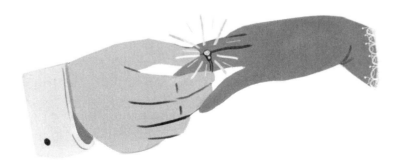

LAWRENCE KOHLBERG'S STAGES OF MORAL DEVELOPMENT

Level I: Preconventional Level

Stage 1—Behave to avoid punishment

Stage 2—Behave to get rewarded

Level II: Conventional Level

Stage 3—Behave based on how others will think about our conduct

Stage 4—Behave based on our understanding of laws and our responsibilities

Level III: Postconventional Level

Stage 5—Behave based on "right thing to do" regardless of personal benefit

Stage 6—Behave based on consistency with "universal ethical principles"

But a few concerning things stuck out to Carol while she was working on this research. The subjects for the research were generally white men or boys. The research did not include any female participants. How could any grand conclusion about such an important facet of the human condition be made when the evidence excluded at least half of the population? It reminded her of when she was a graduate student, and the chairman of her department had told her, "If you add women to your data it just complicates the analysis, so just study men." This seemed like a big problem.

And it wasn't just Kohlberg's research that had such a startling omission, but essentially all research in the field of psychology. In Jean Piaget's classic 1932 book, *Moral Judgement of a Child*, there were four references to the term girl in the index, but none for the term boy—because it was taken for granted that all of the children being discussed were male and the perspectives being described were male. She found this pattern again and again: with Freud, with Erikson, with Kohlberg. No one was including women! One of the only places Carol could even find an acknowledgement of this inequality was in the 1980 *Handbook of Adolescent Psychology*, in which its editor, the psychologist Joseph Adelson, criticized the absence of girls from studies of adolescence. There was very much a missing voice in this most important of conversations.

What Happens When Voices Are Missing?

When voices were left unheard, it reverberated through society. Carol felt this intimately. She felt it when she would read about Freud's belief that women psychologically had no sense of self, as if they were literally "self-less." In a dizzying kind of circular logic, women were being called "selfless" (supposedly a good thing) because they so often assumed the role of serving and caring for others—a role often forced on them by societal norms. But because their "role" was to care for others, they were supposedly also subverting their own self, as if caring for others erased their own identity. In other words, they were being told this was their role while also being told this role resulted in them not having a self.

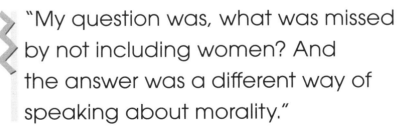 "My question was, what was missed by not including women? And the answer was a different way of speaking about morality."

CAROL GILLIGAN AND THE SEARCH FOR VOICE

She felt the effect of unheard voices when she would hear Erik Erikson, a mentor she respected tremendously, assert that women confused identity with intimacy, as if these two conditions had to be achieved in a specific sequence.

She felt it when she had to try and reconcile her own experience as a parent with what psychology said about infant development—including that infants supposedly couldn't meaningfully connect to other people. But Carol saw how her own infant children absolutely engaged in deep give-and-take relationships with her, with eye contact, physical gestures, and emotional responsiveness. "When I was teaching child development with Erikson, I would put my children to bed and then I would read about mothers and little children," she recalled. "I knew if I drew on my own experience I would get it wrong. So, I had to learn how I was supposed to talk about mothers and young children by reading psychology."

She felt it when she saw how women on average would score lower than men on Lawrence Kohlberg's standards of moral development, when she used the scale in her own research with the Heinz dilemma.

She especially felt it when she received criticism on her own conclusions about moral development. She had emphasized that women tend to morally reason differently than men, that they often strive for an ultimate goal of relationship and empathy rather than a goal of separateness, self-reliance, and honor.

And she even felt it when she was seeking tenure as a professor at Harvard and tended to get a particular type of support from the small group of women members on the faculty. They urged her not to press her argument about psychology's failure to include half the population (women) in their studies. When some of the men on the faculty felt Carol's work was not statistical enough, the chairwoman of her department advised her, "Let them help you. Act as if this makes sense." As Carol would later recall, the message was "let them teach you about regression around the mean, even though it's completely irrelevant to your work and you already know it." This sort of thing was a common strategy that women felt they needed to use to get support from men. Carol thought this kind of thinly veiled game was absurd. "They want to talk with me about methods, they who left out half the sample," she said. But the dean told her not to say anything

"They want to talk with me about methods, they who left out half the sample."

like that. It would just make waves and make things harder for herself. Carol reluctantly agreed. She kept quiet. It was as if Carol heard her mother's voice from the past telling her "What do you know?! Let me tell you how the world works." Carol was basically being told "don't say what you know, don't say what's true about your work. Just play the game." She eventually got tenure in 1986, though she had to compromise some, accomplishing it without a full-throated voice. Her work through the upcoming decades would aim to correct that by using that voice, for herself as well as others.

The Article With a Voice

While at Harvard, Carol wrote an article, mostly for herself, to try and make sense of the dominant voice being used in psychology that she was struggling to relate to. For the article, Carol interviewed pregnant women at various clinics around Boston who were considering whether to have abortions. This was 1975, not long after the U.S. Supreme Court had ruled on the case of Roe v. Wade, which established a woman's reproductive rights and ability to have an abortion (the ruling was overturned by a far more conservative Supreme Court in 2022, fueling heated ideological and

CHAPTER 3

A Discovered Voice

"The failure to see the different reality of women's lives and to hear the differences in their voices stems in part from the assumption that there is a single mode of social experience and interpretation."

Individualism was everything! Or so everyone thought. The common thread in all the most popular developmental psychological models of the time, including those of Freud, Piaget, Erikson, and Kohlberg, was the desire of a person to break away—to separate, to be self-reliant, to achieve autonomy. In short, to become an individual. According to the work of Freud, boys had an extra pull in that direction. Because their mothers were usually their primary caregivers, boys, he said, needed to differentiate themselves from their opposite-gender caregiver in order to establish their own gender-driven identity. Freud said that girls didn't have this same drive to differentiate given that they were the same gender as their primary caregiver. So, according to Freud, girls could just blend in without developing a distinct sense of self.

DID YOU KNOW?

Sigmund Freud might be the most famous name in psychology, but a lot of his ideas were things that we'd probably consider pretty out there now! He didn't understand women very well, going so far as to call them a "dark continent."

Carol rejected this notion on many levels. She did not believe that women fundamentally had an underdeveloped sense of self. She also questioned the basic idea of autonomy and justice being the ultimate universal goals, as Kohlberg's model would suggest. For many people, especially women, relationship, empathy, and connection were the ultimate values to strive for. Why should there be an absolute judgement that somebody is less morally advanced if they value empathy and relationship over autonomy and justice? And, perhaps more importantly, what is the potential risk of always emphasizing autonomy over relationship? Might a cultural bias toward separation and autonomy hinder people's ability to empathize and develop relationships with others? Does it also tend to silence women's true voices? These were the driving themes in that first article of Carol's in the *Harvard Educational Review* in the mid-1970s.

Individualism vs. Empathy

The responses of the women Carol interviewed for *In a Different Voice* showed an entirely different way of thinking about the basis of one's moral judgement. Carol found that the whole issue of choice was very different when considered within a network of relationships. For many women, it was not simply the fetus and the mother who were involved in the dynamic. The decision often involved a network of personal connections, any of whom might potentially be affected by—or affect—the outcome of the woman's decision. Family, friends, and other close acquaintances were all factors here. This kind of decision-making went beyond some kind of universal ideal of right or wrong. It really had little to do with committing an honorable act as an individual. This kind of decision-making was based on a sense of family, community, and relationship. Was this not a completely valid form of moral reasoning?

A few years before she wrote *In a Different Voice*, Carol had been teaching a section of Kohlberg's course on moral reasoning. The Vietnam War was a huge topic at that time. There was a lot of discussion in class about whether the U.S. should've even been involved. Inevitably, the conversation moved to the issue of the mandatory draft by the government and if resisting it based on moral beliefs could be justified or not. The men in the class generally got very quiet when this came up. Carol was fascinated. She sensed that the men were thinking about how a draft would personally and profoundly impact their relationships with their family and friends. Carol suspected that the men's silence was because they worried that if they actually said how they felt, they would sound (according to the beliefs of the time) more like women. They would be prioritizing the value of relationships and care over the value of honor and justice, which would put them at a lower level on Kohlberg's model. So men, too, could struggle with expressing an authentic voice under the pressures and misguided expectations of the wider society.

The Little Book That Started a Revolution

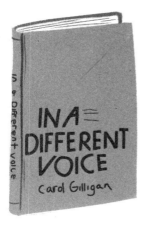

Carol noted this pattern again when she conducted "The College Student Study" on moral and political choice. The study consisted of a randomly chosen group of 25 students who had taken a class on moral and political choice as college sophomores. They were interviewed about their thoughts and attitudes on morality as seniors, and again five years after they graduated. Carol combined the results of that study, the abortion decision study, and a third study, the "right and responsibilities study," which investigated moral judgment and self-perception of men and women ranging in age from 6 to 60 using Kohlberg-like hypothetical moral dilemmas. Ultimately, well over 100 interviews were conducted. The collective outcomes of these three studies made up a book published in 1982 with the same title as that initial research article: *In a Different Voice.* The publisher, Harvard University Press, would go on to refer to it as "the little book that started a revolution."

The main premise of the book, much like the article of the same name, was that when making moral decisions and reasoning through moral dilemmas, men and boys tended to seek the logical, just, and righteous thing to do, whereas women and girls tended to seek the compassionate thing to do that would keep social relationships intact. Women often focused beyond simple individual rights, and more on how to meet the needs of others.

For example, when responding to whether Heinz should steal the medication to save his dying wife, one of the research participants, an 11-year-old boy named Jake remarked, "a human life is worth more than money...the judge would probably think it was the right thing to do." In contrast, an 11-year-old girl named Amy said, "If he stole the drug, he might save his wife then, but if he did, he might have to go to jail and then his wife might get sicker again, and he couldn't get more of the drug...So, they should really talk it out and find some other way to make the money." According to Carol, Amy's response

1984 became the first woman to be a U.S. vice presidential nominee for a major political party, was greatly impacted by Carol's ideas. When Ferraro ran for U.S. Senate in 1992, she regularly mentioned Carol's work in her speeches to voters, emphasizing that women's voices needed to be represented in government.

According to Ferraro's press secretary at the time, Francis Wilkinson, during her Senate campaign one book that Ferraro "clung to like a life raft was *In a Different Voice.*"

During many of those years at Harvard, Carol would go away with her family for the entire summer to Martha's Vineyard. This escape allowed her to get a break from her work and spend valuable time with her husband and their three sons.

 It was not lost on Carol that her home life with her husband and three sons was another setting dominated by the male population. Even the family cat and dog were males!

Her increasingly influential voice needed an occasional rest. But even on vacation, Carol was still surrounded by her work. She was moved by the random encounters she would have with people who would tell her how her book affected their lives. There was the woman behind the counter at the coffee shop who said to Carol, "You explained my marriage." There was the newspaper editor (a man) she ran into on the street who told her, "You explained my divorce." She was receiving letters from all over the world, from people of all walks of life. They were thanking her for the impact *In a Different Voice* had on them.

Legal experts even began reconsidering basic law as a result of Carol's work. For example, what if a

potentially illegal act were committed based on an Ethic of Care? Should that factor into the judgement of a defendant's innocence or guilt? Also, as an increasing number of women were becoming lawyers and judges, would that change the way the law would ultimately be interpreted? Would it introduce a different voice into the law? Although these questions could not be clearly answered, one thing was clear; Carol's ideas were being taken seriously across all of society. This eventually included the highest court in the land, as U.S. Supreme Court Justice Sonia Sotomayor referenced Carol's work in her writings and speeches.

The honors and accolades kept coming. In 1992, Carol was appointed as professor at the University of Cambridge in England, where she taught through 1994, and was awarded the prestigious Grawemeyer Award in Education, which honors achievements in fields not recognized by the Nobel prizes, such as education and music. That same year, a book Carol wrote with her graduate student Lyn Mikel Brown, *Meeting at the Crossroads*, about adolescent girls silencing their own voices based on external pressures, became a *New York Times* Notable Book. And to top it off, Carol's work was widely cited as influencing the passing of the 1993 federal Gender Equity in Education Act, requiring equal opportunities, treatment, and respect for boys and girls in school settings and activities. This included things like equal encouragement of math and science programs for girls and boys, programs to more effectively address sexual harassment, and dropout prevention programs for pregnant and parenting teenagers.

In the early 1990s, Marie C. Wilson, president of the Ms. Foundation for Women, a feminist organization associated with *Ms.* Magazine, teamed up with the magazine's co-founder, Gloria Steinem. They wanted girls to envision a boundless future where they could be whomever they wanted, and find comfortable and welcoming opportunities in the workplace. They wanted girls to feel confident and empowered. Wilson openly acknowledged that this vision was inspired by Carol Gilligan's research highlighting how adolescent girls struggled with their sense of self and thinking and saying what they really felt. This idea evolved into dedicating a day of the year where girls could have a direct experience in different work environments to get a sense of what professional options were out there. Parents and guardians would be invited to give their girls a taste of the working world. The day would occur on the fourth Thursday of every April. And so, the first Take Our Daughters to Work Day occurred on April 22, 1993. By 1996, five million girls in 14 countries were taking part in this event. Carol's work had provided fertile ground for the voices of girls and young women to blossom throughout the world.

In 1996, Carol was included among *Time* magazine's 25 Most Influential People. She became the first head of the new Gender Studies department at Harvard's Graduate School of Education, a program she helped establish, in 1997. In 1998, she received the prestigious $250,000 Heinz Award in the Human Condition for her ability to "transform the paradigm of what it means to be human." By the end of the 1990s, Carol was receiving enormous amounts of attention. So much of it was extremely positive. But there was another side to it—a side that wanted to quiet that thriving voice.

TRY THIS

Moral Dilemmas

Read each of the following scenarios. As you do, think about:

> How can this be answered to get to the Postconventional level according to Lawrence Kohlberg's Ethic of Justice model from Chapter 2?

> How can this be answered to get to the Postconventional level according to Carol Gilligan's Ethic of Care model?

> What do you think you would most likely do in this scenario?

Scenario 1: Natalie is a high school senior and editor-in-chief of her school newspaper. She takes the responsibilities of her job very seriously. A few students at the school have started publicly claiming that administrators have been ignoring flagrant bullying incidents at the school. They want Natalie to run a story about it in the newspaper. Natalie is torn between her responsibility to print important school news and the risk of getting in trouble with the administration. What should Natalie do?

Scenario 2: Michelle and Henry are both high school juniors. They have been in an exclusive relationship for eight months. Max is good friends with both of them. One day while Max is at the diner with his family he notices Henry sitting at a table in the corner kissing another girl. What should Max do about what he has observed? Should he tell Michelle?

Scenario 3: Andre is a high school senior. His parents are very strict. They are going out for the evening and tell Andre he has to stay home and study. Instead, Andre waits until they leave to go to a party where there will be no adults and there will be underage drinking going on. He figures he will stay for a short amount of time and then go home before his parents are back. Although Andre does not consume any alcohol himself at the party, his best friend, Jeff, gets drunk and pleads with Andre to give him a ride home. If he agrees to drive Jeff, Andre is going to get home after his parents have already returned, creating a potentially big problem for himself with his parents. What should Andre do?

CHAPTER 4

A Challenged Voice

"Rather than asking, how do we gain the capacity to care, the questions become, how do we come not to care, how do we lose the capacity for empathy and mutual understanding?"

"The hardest times for me are not when people challenged what I said, but when I felt my voice was not heard."

Over the course of the 1990s, Carol had made her mark, becoming a widely acclaimed figure in the field of psychology and in society as a whole. She had most definitely found her voice, and in doing so had helped change the field of psychology by casting a light on the absent or misplaced voices of other women. She was being recognized for her positive contributions. But as she continued to rack up the honors, the criticisms of Carol and her work started slowly mounting as well. Carol's ideas rubbed some people the wrong way—on both sides of the ideological spectrum.

Too Feminist?

There were some who dismissed Carol's work because of her feminism. They claimed that her work was automatically unscientific and politically motivated, as if one couldn't be a feminist and scientist at the same time. There were even some who believed she was trying to turn boys into girls.

In her 2000 book, *The War Against Boys*, socially conservative author Christina Hoff Sommers argued that boys were being unfairly portrayed as the favored gender in society and that this favoritism created barriers for girls when in fact, according to Sommers, it was boys who were struggling in school, among other facets of society, more than girls. In the book, Carol was singled out as one of the main culprits of this supposed anti-boy narrative (though even Sommers acknowledged positive aspects of Carol's work with girls: that educators and parents were now paying more attention to the importance of math and science for girls and how there was more support for girls to participate in sports).

In 2003, Take Our Daughters to Work Day was officially expanded to include boys and renamed Take Our Daughters and Sons to Work Day, after a great deal of pushback on the fact that boys had not been included. There was even a lawsuit in 2002 brought by a men's-rights activist alleging gender discrimination against boys. Although the lawsuit was dismissed because the plaintiff had no basis in claiming he was personally harmed, the organization ultimately agreed to the more inclusive change in 2003. But some people felt changing it was getting away from the original intent of the program. It seemed a backlash against feminism and a move to dilute the very voices that the program aimed to lift up.

Not Feminist Enough?

On the other side of the spectrum, some feminists were slamming Carol for allegedly reinforcing outdated stereotypes that women tend to be highly sensitive and play more of a caretaking role by nature, often referred to as essentialism. Women had fought long and hard to assert themselves in the workplace and in most other spaces in society. These particular feminists feared that ideas like Carol's could set them back and send counterproductive messages that all women were more innately prone to be nurturers and take on traditional roles. Unfortunately, this interpretation revealed a fundamental misunderstanding of her work. Carol never intended to be defining a singular experience for all women. It was more complicated than that.

Not Scientific Enough?

There was also still the same old argument about how her research methods were not scientific enough and therefore her conclusions lacked validity. She would later reflect, "They said my work was not psychology, the department in which I have more graduate students than anyone. My students were getting their dissertations published by Harvard Press but my work wasn't taught by my colleagues. In the committee on degrees, my students were being told that their research isn't science." These mixed messages from the academic community about Carol's work were just one more hurdle to overcome.

Where Was All This Coming From?

How did Carol respond to all this? Well, one way she did not respond was to be openly defensive. She chose to stay above the fray and not get involved with back-and-forth debates about any of these issues. She was annoyed by others' attempts to distort her work by describing it as something it wasn't. "It's a caricature of my book that gets attacked," she once said. It was as if these critics were speaking for her, but doing so using a voice that was not hers—another type of ventriloquism.

Most of the criticisms, in Carol's view, stemmed from patriarchy. Patriarchy is a way society is organized that creates an artificial set of rules, codes, and messages that indicate how men and women, and boys and girls, should act and be in the world. It is a system set up to value some men above other men, such as white men over men of color or straight men over gay men, and all men above women. When people claimed that she was part of some alleged war against boys, she would remind them that she had just as much concern for the well-being and mental health of boys as she did girls. When speaking about the perils of patriarchy, she insisted that "in essence, patriarchy harms both men and women by forcing men to act as if they don't have or need relationships and women to act as if they don't have or need a self." To Carol, both men and women, and boys and girls, were at social and emotional risk in this kind of system.

> Patriarchy harms both men and women by forcing men to act as if they don't have or need relationships and women to act as if they don't have or need a self.

As to the feminist critics, they seemed to be misinterpreting Carol's claims of varying voices as a statement that there is a specifically masculine voice that represents accomplishment and a feminine voice that tries to merely maintain relationships. Carol would get frustrated when people would assume she was speaking of voices in some oversimplified and rigid gender binary between masculine traits and feminine traits. Titling her landmark book *In a Different Voice* was a conscious decision. If she thought of that other voice as strictly a feminine voice, she might have called the book *"In a Woman's Voice."* "The different voice I describe is characterized not by gender but by theme," she maintained instead. That is to say, if one is thinking of this long-neglected "different voice" as a woman's voice, it is only because the patriarchal system we all live in tells us to think of it that way. Carol really wanted to highlight the fact that people do not speak with a single voice nor follow a single path toward social and moral development. If we think of this idea within the framework of a democratic and more equitable system, this different voice is simply a human voice.

Carol also preferred to avoid the age-old nature vs. nurture debate when trying to explain why women and men tend to be different from one another in terms of behavior, self-identity, and voice. It was beside the point to Carol whether these tendencies stemmed more from our biologically programmed nature or more from the nurturing by social and environmental influences. For Carol, these questions were more suited for biologists or sociologists. Psychology's consideration of the human condition was as much an art as a science.

The question of whether her research was scientific enough was another issue that she found to be an empty distraction. Most traditional psychological studies are tightly designed, with participants in controlled environments being asked to complete specific tasks. The participants often enter the research setting without knowing much about the study, like whether they are in an experimental group or a control group, or sometimes even what the point of the study actually is. This reduces the likelihood that people's ideas about what should happen during the study will influence the results. Sometimes the studies are "double-blind," which means neither the participants nor the researchers know who is in what group! Carol's research, on the other hand, was usually based on interviews with people in their regular everyday world. She preferred to work within more natural circumstances in order to best draw out the participants' most authentic voices.

Carol maintained that her research was legitimate, much of it published in several peer-reviewed books and top journals in the field of developmental psychology

DID YOU KNOW?

Charles Darwin's famous journey to the Galapagos is what inspired his book *The Origin of Species,* and the theory of evolution.

with strict editorial standards. "Science is to argue from evidence. And my work is inductive," she once said. Plus, as she once pointed out, if quantitative studies were the only kind of valid research, then Charles Darwin, the forefather of evolutionary biology, would not be considered a researcher. Carol saw herself as pursuing a Darwinian method of inquiry. She was inspired by his book, *Voyage of the Beagle*, which documented his important work simply watching birds and iguanas on the Galapagos Islands. He didn't set up any fancy experiments, just observed these creatures move within their natural environments, noting how they made adaptations along the way. She loosely compared her own research to Darwin's, saying "I went to my own version of the Galapagos Islands with a group of colleagues…We traveled to girls in search of the origins of women's development."

> "I went to my own version of the Galapagos Islands with a group of colleagues…We traveled to girls in search of the origins of women's development."

The Listening Guide Method

Carol's methodology relied heavily on the interview process and active listening, which allowed the interviewee's answers to help guide the direction of the questions. This more personal form of interviewing made it possible for the subjects to speak about what they knew to be true in their worlds, and for those conducting the research to best understand them. Carol felt that this method was appropriate for her mission and the purposes of her work. She would eventually go on to develop an original and influential interviewing system reflecting her personal approach called the "Listening Guide Method." She insisted that following some kind of specific set of research methods would be giving in to the standards of the very patriarchal system, which she viewed as the problem. She resisted the need to defend her methods by quoting the feminist poet Audre Lorde: "The master's tools will never dismantle the master's house." Carol was always quite comfortable conducting her work out of the box and on the edge. She would continue to contend that her work was scientific, maybe just not the type of science others thought acceptable. There were plenty of other ways to do genuine scientific research that didn't necessarily include a double-blind study or an experimental group and a control group or any other similarly rigid methodology.

Any of the criticisms of Carol over statistics and science also seemed to be serving another purpose. Claiming that somebody's work was scientifically invalid could be taken as a form of telling her that her voice was not wanted in the conversation. Another attempt at muting Carol's voice. And it was a type of silencing that continued to happen all too often to both girls and boys.

Carol dove further into the buried voices of young people. With some other faculty members at Harvard, Carol had started the Harvard Project on Women's Psychology, Boys' Development and the Culture of Manhood, which conducted important research for years. Through this project she picked up on a disturbing pattern that seemed to occur in both girls and boys, though at different ages.

What Happens to Girls' Voices?

Carol found that girls tended to lose their assertive voice as they approached their adolescent years. Before adolescence, they would generally present as much more feisty, straight-talking, and emotionally honest. Then something changed as they became teenagers. Iris, a high school student Carol interviewed, said "If I were to say what I was feeling and thinking, no one would want to be with me, my voice would be too loud." As girls become adolescents, they seem to think that they have to censor themselves to be more socially appealing to others, or else people might not want to be around them. Carol thought this moment in a girl's life was pivotal—and a sad sign that they felt that in order to fit in, they had to quiet their voice, or even lose it.

This kind of self-censorship could leave a person at risk for feelings of hopelessness, anxiety, and depression. And according to Carol's research, this was not the only thing many teenage girls lost. They also lost the ability to "know what they know." They basically were learning to forget that they could have their own ideas and instead would rely on outside authority to tell them what to think. This was something Carol herself had experienced on many occasions in her younger years. When the teenage girls she interviewed would reply "I don't know" to questions about their own opinion and voice, Carol heard something more, something

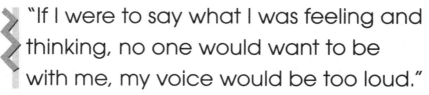

"If I were to say what I was feeling and thinking, no one would want to be with me, my voice would be too loud."

beneath the surface. Many of these young women weren't simply being dismissive or apathetic. "I don't know" seemed to signify some kind of self-rejection and lapse in self-confidence about their own knowledge. They were putting the word "don't" in the middle of their ability to know what they know.

Judy was a thirteen-year-old girl participating in one of Carol's research studies through the Harvard Project. In her interview, Judy talked about losing deep and meaningful social connections being like "forgetting your mind." Judy said that the mind was "associated with your heart and your soul and your internal feelings and your real feelings." This was in contrast with the brain, which she suggested was located in one's head and dealt with intelligence and education. So Judy was implying that when we separate out our feelings from our intelligence we are essentially "losing our minds." Like Iris, Judy seemed to be describing how teenage girls tended to censor themselves in order to conform to some artificial standard. Carol was impressed by this insight and folded Judy's perceptive observation into her own ideas about the loss of voice by noting "When we separate our minds from our bodies, we are in danger of forgetting our mind—that is, forgetting what we know in our hearts and our souls." Carol added "when we forget our minds, we lose touch with ourselves, and thereby lose the capacity to be in relationship."

Carol saw more cultural evidence of the patriarchy shutting down voices in many of the books she loved, including *The Bluest Eye* by Toni Morrison, Charlotte Bronte's *Jane Eyre*, *Oedipus Rex* by Sophocles, and *The Diary of Anne Frank*. In Anne Frank's writing the author even admits that she often used a muffled voice in her everyday life, with such entries as: "I never utter my real feelings about anything," "If I'm to be quite honest, then I must admit that it does hurt me," and "A voice within me is sobbing."

The tendency for young women to value relationships created something of a paradox. In order to connect with others, teenage girls often felt they had to take a big part of themselves out of their relationships. They felt they had to censor themselves and silence their voices so that others wouldn't find them too overbearing or too loud or too weird. And when girls sought relationships with muffled voices, they were likely developing inauthentic and less meaningful relationships. So, while they might have friendships, Carol wondered how deep and real those friendships actually were when they weren't using their true, full voices.

And What About Boys' Voices?

Boys had a somewhat different timetable. According to Carol's work with her former graduate student Judy Chu, boys tended to experience a change sometime between the ages of four and seven, at which time they started losing their expressive voice. Carol noted that "for over 100 years, researchers have been observing that girls are more resilient than boys in childhood." Carol wanted to find out more. She thought that even at such a young age, boys seemed to show early signs of not wanting to be too flamboyant or emotional, to avoid being thought of as weak or girly, a potential bruise to their masculinity. They wanted to avoid being teased or bullied. But what was the cost of this protective shell for young boys?

As part of the research for her 2002 book *The Birth of Pleasure*, Carol was observing a group of four-year-old boys interacting in their preschool class. She had been so moved by the affection and love expressed by many of the boys toward their fathers during morning drop-offs. The tenderhearted hugs reflected pure love between the boys and their parents. She proceeded to carefully watch as a few of the boys ended up in the classroom's dress-up corner. One of the boys picked up a piece of pink lace and drew attention to it. One of the other boys was holding a Lego construction in the shape of a gun and started instructing the other boys, "Come on, you guys. Help me bring these animals to the hideout. We're blowing things up, we're the bad guys."

A few days later she conducted another observation of the four-year-olds' free play. One of the boys seemed to pick up from where they left off last time by holding a stuffed bunny by the ear in one hand and another Lego gun in the other before saying "Hey, let's go, partner, let's go." The combination of the bunny and the toy gun seem to be capturing a profound moment in time. It was as if a sudden transformation had happened between one hand to the next; from bunny to gun; from gentle and caring to rough and tough. Another boy put on a cape and said "I'm a bank robber, too, in disguise." A third boy then cut in "I'm gonna shoot, shoot the bad guys." The boy holding the bunny then replied, "we're the bad guys."

As Carol took in these interactions she had a distinct sense that the boys' voices were following some kind of script. She was taken by the contrast between the visible displays of affection shown toward their fathers and their subsequent play featuring more aggressive themes. She couldn't help but feel she was watching these four-year-olds at a major turning point in their lives. They seemed to be moving away from affection and toward fulfilling the expectations of how they should act as boys based on scripts and narratives from the outside world.

Before this change, the boys seemed to possess extremely authentic and articulate voices. They had no problem expressing their love for their fathers at drop off. They didn't care what colors or toys were "for boys" or "for girls." Carol recounted a five year-old boy saying, "Mommy, why do you smile when you're sad?," a warm gesture that demonstrated an attentiveness to emotion and a sensitive reading of the world. Then around kindergarten and first grade, this type of sensitivity and expression started to fade as young boys often became increasingly inauthentic, indirect, and inarticulate. As this shift commonly occurs, boys often begin to withhold their personal feelings and opinions. When one observed young boy accidentally bumped his head against a table in

his classroom and openly exclaimed, "Ow! I hit my head," one of the adults came over to offer assistance, caringly asking "You hit your head? Uh-oh. Are you OK?" The boy aggravatedly responded, "Don't say that! I'm all right. I don't care if I hit my head." The boy seemed to be shutting down his true thoughts and feelings in order to present an image of being tough and strong. Carol interviewed some of the fathers who were concerned that their young sons might lose their tenderness, expressiveness, and closeness with friends. But ironically, many of these fathers were contributing to that very silencing of voice in their sons, even if they didn't realize it. When a young boy was encouraged to not show too much emotion or else he wouldn't be "acting like a man," were they not being influenced to lose an important part of their voice? Did this early loss of voice in boys have something to do with how so many young men later experienced mental health challenges (like depression, anxiety, or excessive anger) without seeking adequate help?

Both the beginning of adolescence and the end of early childhood are notable times of significant physical development, cognitive and emotional growth, and new experiences. Carol thought that this potential muting of the boys' voices at such a young age was probably related to the muting of the girls' voices in adolescence.

In Carol's words, "To put it very concretely: when a boy cries and is then laughed at or shunned, or when a girl says what she actually feels and thinks and is then excluded, their encounter with the codes and scripts of patriarchal manhood and womanhood registers as a rupture of relationship." That is: when boys and girls unwittingly follow the rules of patriarchy, relationships can suffer.

Journal Prompt

Have you ever felt the need to suppress your true voice in order to fit in? Maybe you've pretended to like a movie or an activity that your friends like. Or maybe you worry that your ideas aren't good enough. Do you think anyone you know might also sometimes suppress themselves in order to fit in? If so, maybe try an experiment (a casual one, like Darwin & Carol's!) and next time you aren't completely feeling an idea, speak up! Chances are, others will appreciate your voice.

CHAPTER 5

A Reclaimed Voice

"As the healthy body resists infection, so the healthy psyche resists the loss of voice and the loss of relationship."

"I see the release of a human voice that is direct and compassionate as a progression toward democracy."

2002 was a big year for Carol. She left Harvard after decades of teaching and researching there to become a professor at New York University. As a native New Yorker, it felt like coming home. She had spent time in 1998 teaching as a visiting professor at NYU law school, which she loved. She described NYU as having "a wider intellectual sky" than what she had become used to at Harvard. When Carol arrived in 2002, she began to concentrate on the theme of healthy resistance to those forces that attempted to shut down one's voice. She began teaching graduate courses such as "Resisting Injustice." Combining elements of literature, law, art, and psychology, Carol's classes were filled with students from across disciplines—even law students! She continued to discover fresh and interesting ways to blend her many passions, finding intersections across diverse fields and using them to create new ways of thinking about people, their voices, and their need to feel connections with others. One of her department chairmen at Harvard had once tried to criticize her by saying, "Your work is not science. It's poetry." And she thought, "Well, that's a compliment."

She continually added new vocabulary to more completely describe her ideas. Each new key term that she adopted, whether it be voice, patriarchy, resistance, democracy, or trauma, was like a fresh coat of paint making the details of her points all the more vivid. She had come to think of herself as more of an "artist-psychologist."

One year before her move to NYU, as she was preparing to make the move from Boston to New York City, the Harvard Graduate School of Education was preparing to launch the Harvard Center of Gender and Education. Plans to set it up were made possible by a $12.5 million gift from Carol's good friend, the Oscar-winning actress and committed feminist Jane Fonda. Fonda had been strongly inspired by Carol's work. She once said during a speech at Harvard, "I know what Professor Gilligan writes about. I know it in my skin, in my gut, as well as in my voice."

> "I know what Professor Gilligan writes about. I know it in my skin, in my gut, as well as in my voice."

The center would explore how children's development and learning were influenced by gender. At the announcement about the center and the donation in 2001, Fonda said, "I'm grateful to be able to do this for my sister, my friend, Carol Gilligan." Unfortunately, the center was not able to become a reality due to subsequent logistical issues, but it was clear that Carol's compelling voice and giant reputation were reverberating throughout society.

The True Ventriloquist

Carol kept exploring the negative effects of patriarchy on a society. As she once pointed out, "If you want to elevate one group of people over another you have to undercut our relational capacities as human beings." This was one of the big problems of patriarchy, from her point of view. "You have to stop the person at the top from feeling empathy for the people at the bottom," she said. The way some people ended up above other people could be based on a variety of factors, including race, socioeconomic status, sexual identity, disability, and, of course, gender. Patriarchy served to divide people and keep them disconnected from one another. This seemed like a harmful way to shape a society whose goals should include good citizenship, community-building, equal rights and opportunities,

DID YOU KNOW?

Parents today are advised not to spend too much time staring at their phones around their infants, not just for the obvious reasons, but also because of the Still-Face experiment! Babies have negative reactions to blank stares on adults' faces...which is usually the face we make when we're scrolling mindlessly!

though there was a temporary break in the relationship between mother and baby, they were able to swiftly repair it and restore the harmony. This reinforced for Carol that relationships between people may not always be smooth, but they can be improved upon even in the wake of upsetting interactions. Another point Carol picked up on was the baby's increasingly desperate attempts to re-engage with the mother once she stopped showing emotion. Carol thought this carried a particularly powerful message regarding an attentiveness to the signals given off by others: "From this we learn that by paying attention to changes in posture and listening for changes in voice, we can pick up and follow the moves in and out of relationship," she concluded. This seemed like another illustration of the importance of listening for the voice underneath the voice and the story beneath the story.

Eric Tronick's "Still-Face experiment" was a stark example of what can happen when there is an overemphasis on separation and independence, occurring as early as our first year of life. The baby's reaction seemed to be a preliminary form of healthy resistance—just like Carol's own early resistance during that summer at Vassar when she did not take well to being separated from her mother at bedtime. Carol saw the experiment as if infants, the youngest among us, were pointing the way in telling us what we all truly need. And when we don't get what we need from the system surrounding us, we resist that system. These voices of distress were actually expressions of hope, under the surface. Hope for women to authentically communicate their thoughts and feelings. Hope for men to embrace their emotional needs in order to realize more well-rounded and deeper forms of themselves. Those young cries of resistance were soaring reminders of what it meant to be fully human.

The story of voice has always underscored the story of Carol Gilligan's life and work. Now in her mid-eighties, Carol continues to teach at NYU and is still actively writing new books. Hers is a story that clearly continues to unfold.

Listening Guide Method

Listen for Plot

Listen for the "I"

Listen for Conflicted Voices

Think about the last time a friend or family member talked to you about something serious. What kind of listener were you? Did you follow any of these guidelines, even without realizing? Could you use them the next time someone needs to talk to you about something important?

An Echoing Voice

"The different voice is a voice for the 21st century."

Carol Gilligan's lifetime devotion to discovering and understanding the human voice has had a monumental influence across fields as diverse as psychology, law, education, and business. A variety of policies and practices later adopted in these fields capture many of Carol's ideas. Ideas of hers once considered fairly radical eventually were much more in line with the mainstream. The passage of time has a way of nudging the culture toward self-correction. Carol laid the groundwork for so many subsequent trends and movements. Here are just a few areas in which Carol's work has made an enduring impact:

Emotional Intelligence

In schools, the importance of thinking about the "whole student" gained steady momentum during the latter decades of the 20th century and into the 2000s. The idea of nurturing children's social, emotional, and moral well-being just as much as building their reading, writing, and math skills became a priority. There was a growing recognition that when teachers built caring relationships with the students in their classrooms, the students were better off academically as well as socially and emotionally. Books such as *Reviving Ophelia: Saving the Selves of Adolescent Girls* by Mary Pipher, and *Emotional Intelligence* by Daniel

Goleman became runaway bestsellers in the 1990s. Both books owed a great deal to Carol Gilligan.

Carol's work served as a foundation to these increasingly popular topics. Her claim that the act of connecting reason with emotion is the act of using a true voice, a human voice, lingers in all of the subsequent work on this subject. The emotional fragility of teenagers and the overall social-emotional development of all young people became paramount issues across society. And these concerns have grown even more relevant with the eruption of social media at the beginning of the 2000s and its apparent impacts on the mental health of young people.

By the early 2000s, most U.S. states had implemented Social Emotional Learning standards in their schools, with an emphasis on skills like self-awareness, self-management, social awareness, relationship-building, and responsible decision-making. Sound familiar? Carol was there decades earlier, talking about these capabilities, offering methods to enhance the internal lives of young people, and warning about the continued risks if they were not properly addressed. It could be said she changed the direction of the conversation, and in doing so changed history.

Diversity, Equity, and Inclusion Movements

Diversity, Equity, and Inclusion initiatives are commonly practiced in schools, community organizations, and workplaces. They recognize the importance of creating environments that welcome and acknowledge people of all kinds of backgrounds. Research shows that businesses are often more successful when there is more diversity among their employees, and that students benefit academically and socially when there is more diversity in their classrooms. Schools across the country include lessons on the contributions and experiences of individuals with diverse abilities, cultures, and identities in their curricula. It's a way to help students develop empathy and understanding

DID YOU KNOW?

Many workplaces now have whole DEI taskforces or departments to specifically try and make sure the company is representing and supporting a broad range of voices.

for one another, and for everyone to feel represented. It is ultimately a celebration of voices.

Carol widely received credit when the Gender Equity in Education Act passed in 1993, which promoted educational policies specifically related to gender. It provided millions of dollars for new equity-based programming and curriculum development, with a focus on enhancing the participation and achievement of girls.

There has certainly been progress regarding work opportunities for women over the years spanning Carol's career. Studies have found that between 1970 and 2009, 38 million more women entered the workforce in the U.S.—and that those 38 million women were responsible for the economy being 25% bigger than it would have been without them. That is significant, but there is further to go. There is still a troubling gender wage gap. Even as recently as 2020, women on average earned only 82 cents for every dollar a man earned for the same work, according to information from the Bureau of Labor Statistics. Women have also continued to be vastly underrepresented in the fields of science, technology, engineering, and math (STEM). When certain groups of people aren't sufficiently represented in an industry, the unique perspective that group can offer is lost.

This kind of exclusion can even be dangerous. An example you might not know about: when seatbelts were first invented, they were designed primarily with men in mind. And women were actually more likely to die in car accidents because the designs didn't fit them well! For a long time, manufacturers had relied solely on adult male crash test dummies to ensure the safety of their products. Now, engineers use female crash test dummies in the driver's seat as well, to help reduce the incidence of fatal and severe injuries to women. It was a lot like Carol's warnings about the omission of women in psychology—it was irresponsible, and potentially harmful. And people eventually took notice.

Carol keenly understood that a diversity of voices was a necessary ingredient to a well-functioning society.

"Smash The Patriarchy"

When Carol titled her book with the question *Why Does Patriarchy Persist?*, it seemed like the world gave her a collective response in the form of a social media meme: #SmashthePatriarchy became a rallying cry for millions of people. Carol had been talking for decades about the deep problems with patriarchy as a system of power that shuts down voices, favors men over women, and devalues the spirit of relationships and community. She saw it as just as harmful to men as it was to women. For too long, patriarchy had been incorrectly interpreted as a mere reflection of nature—how things inherently are biologically, rather than the constructed social system that it is. Her ongoing efforts to resist this particular form of oppression, both in her work and her life, finally seemed to be catching on as the Smash the Patriarchy movement emerged from a rousing chorus of voices. Adopted as a feminist call to action, especially among young people, Smash the Patriarchy steadily became a concise and assertive social and political statement. The phrase seemed to be showing up everywhere: on T-shirts, social media videos, bumper stickers, and signs at political rallies. Even pop music superstar Taylor Swift got in on the action with a slightly more col-orful take on the slogan in a 2021 re-released version of her hit song "All Too Well."

AN ECHOING VOICE *

DID YOU KNOW?

Even Barbie is in on it! The 2023 Blockbuster movie Barbie had a particularly clever take on both the concept of patriarchy, and on what happens when certain voices are neglected.

For decades, Carol had been emphasizing the need for resistant voices, and now many of those voices seemed to be breaking through into popular culture in a big way.

Trauma-Informed Practices

By the 2000s, the reality of trauma and its potential impact on young people had become a much more widely discussed issue. New research showed both emotional and physical risks to those who experienced early childhood trauma, whether it was exposure to domestic violence, emotional abuse, the death of a loved one, or any other major adverse event. A Stanford University study revealed that early exposure to trauma could affect the development of the hippocampus, a region in the brain related to memory. A separate study by the Centers for Disease Control found a link between childhood trauma and an increased chance of certain diseases in adulthood, including diabetes, heart disease, and even specific types of cancer, in addition to social and emotional challenges.

As this research continued to come to light, schools across the U.S. started putting more trauma-informed practices into place. This included greater training for school staffs on identifying warning signs and possible emotional and academic effects on students who might have experienced trauma. As a result, teachers have been gaining a clearer understanding of the kind of student who might seem like someone who willfully *won't* do in the classroom but might actually be someone who desperately *can't* do—yet another time to listen for the story beneath the story. Many schools have also been expanding mental health services within their buildings by hiring more psychologists, social workers, and counselors. Some good news in the research is that if students receive prompt and effective help in coping with their early childhood trauma, there is a reversal in the risks to their long-term psychological and physical health. Carol Gilligan, once again proving to be on the cutting edge, anticipated the risks of trauma and the disruption of vital relationships. Her early research on the Ethic of Care as well as her later work with the Radical Listening project at NYU emphasized the importance of maintaining trusting relationships and carefully listening to the voices of those who had experienced trauma.

Studies on Happiness

A Harvard University study that began in 1938 by following around 700 students has continued over the decades to include more than 1,300 people over three generations. The participants have rated the quality of their lives by completing questionnaires on their levels of happiness. According to this extensive study, the healthiest and happiest people have had one major factor in common: Good relationships. Carol had been talking about the deep human need for relationships since her original research in the 1970s. As accumulated research seems to indicate, happiness most commonly and abundantly springs from a feeling of relationships and connectedness with others. A sense of individuality and independence, of course, can help boost one's self-esteem. But too much emphasis on relying primarily on oneself can lead to feelings of isolation and loneliness. Carol understood this.

A 2021 survey from the CDC of thousands of teenagers in the U.S. found that a disturbingly high 57% of teenage girls had reported persistent feelings of sadness or hopelessness. The percentage of boys reporting the same feelings was 29%—not as high as the girls, but still a concerning number. While the report could not provide the exact reasons behind these alarming numbers, the COVID-19 pandemic surely had something to do with it. One of the more troubling legacies of the COVID pandemic was the detrimental effects that the social isolation had on the population as a whole, and especially young people. This took a toll on the mental health of many children

and adolescents. Another cause for this troubling trend identified by the CDC was almost certainly related to the more toxic effects of social media. Social media sites are too often platforms for young people to display inauthentic and overly idealized versions of themselves, in terms of their lifestyles, their physical appearances, or even their emotional states. Too often, they are projecting voices on these platforms that are not really their own. We can come back again to Carol's defining point throughout her work on the loss of voice: Mental health is closely tied to voice, and when one's voice is not truly realized, crisis too often follows.

Restorative Disciplinary Practices

Another big pivot that was taking place by the early 2000s was the way in which schools were approaching their disciplinary policies. Traditionally, schools tended to rely primarily on punishments for student misbehavior. These included things like detentions, suspensions, and in some extreme cases expulsion. But research showed that these are generally not very effective methods for discouraging misconduct. Responding to negative behaviors only with negative consequences ignored the deeper meaning of those behaviors. An alternative form of discipline arose in schools. It is commonly referred to as restorative discipline.

A restorative approach likens a misbehavior to a rip in the fabric of a school community. It encourages a more democratic solution than simply punishing the wrongdoer; it focuses on repairing the damage. This could be by having the student write a sincere letter of apology acknowledging the impact of their actions. Or it could be having the student perform some act of community service within the school, like helping out in a classroom of younger students. The main point is that they would need to give back to the school community in some positive and productive way.

There is emerging research that shows a decrease in repeated misbehaviors for students who were given strong restorative consequences. This change of policy seems to reflect a shift away from a strict ethic of justice (through punitive measures)...and towards an ethic of care. This approach really demonstrates the spirit of Carol's desire to break democracy free from patriarchy. It is a spirit that raises the voices of individual students—while at the same time boosting the collective voice of an entire school community.

Gender Identity Fluidity

One of Carol's frustrations was the incorrect assumption often made that through her work she was declaring the existence of a separate male voice and female voice. This was not what she was saying. Did she think there was a tendency for women to more commonly lean toward relationships in their moral decision-making and men more commonly toward justice in theirs? Yes. But, did she think that many women considered justice in their reasoning and that many men considered relationships in their reasoning? Absolutely! Again, Carol's "different voice" was a universally human voice, one that could belong to both women and men. In fact, Carol believed it was the system of patriarchy that insisted on thinking of men and woman as having voices and attitudes as distinctly separate from one another. For Carol, if patriarchy could be overcome, the commonalities across genders could be better appreciated and celebrated.

And there's been a movement in that direction since the early 2000s. Across society there has been increasing acceptance of gender not as a binary, but as a spectrum, and of individuals who identify at various points on that spectrum. It is the humanity of the person that matters most, not whether they identify as a man or a woman. For these folks grappling with their sense of identity, an expanding social acceptance of the way we think about gender categories could only be refreshingly liberating. When society accepts that some

people might not fit into a rigid classification, those people are likely to feel a greater sense of belonging in the world. And, in some cases, this wider acceptance may even be saving lives.

There is growing appreciation for a broader and more self-empowering diversity in how people are identifying themselves across the LGBTQ+ community. In the past, the constraints of using strictly binary modes to identify themselves left many young people in clouds of despair and isolation. Since then, gender expression has been allowed to take a richer and more accepting range of non-binary forms, allowing people to more fully embrace who they are at their cores.

Carol Gilligan's encouragement of discovering one's unique voice despite the often stifling forces imposed by society echo in the movement that led a great many people to identify and express themselves more fully and authentically. Hopefully the world is a more welcoming place for them as they move through their lives. This change will likely remain a topic of debate for years to come. But it seems clear the shift in perspective is countering unnecessary cruelty while helping an enormous number of people feel more seen, and their voices more genuinely heard.

#MeToo Movement

By the mid-2010s there was another highly visible movement that surged through the culture. Hollywood became an epicenter for taking a deeper look into the persistent problem of sexual harassment and intimidation, particularly at the workplace. This issue had long troubled the consciousness of society. In 1991, during the Supreme Court confirmation hearings of Clarence Thomas, the world was enthralled by the televised hearings of Anita Hill. Hill accused Thomas of sexually harassing her while she worked for him

years earlier. Her claims were shocking and upsetting. The country seemed torn on whether or not she
was telling the truth. One of the most unforgettable
aspects of Hill's testimony was the series of follow-up
questions she had to sit through by the mostly white
and male members of the Senate judiciary committee.
The questions were deeply personal, judgmental, and
humiliating. For many who believed she was telling
the truth, the personal and confrontational questions
being fired at her felt like she was being re-victimized.
Carol felt strongly about Anita Hill's testimony. In

a 1994 article in the *Fordham Law Review*, Carol recounted how Hill's "voice was filtered through the responses of the senators and their expert witnesses. I remembered the two-step process of listening to Anita Hill—hearing her, and then hearing her not being heard." Unfortunately, this demeaning treatment of women who try to project their voices in cases of harassment and abuse has been an ongoing struggle that has long served as a barrier to victims coming forward.

Then, the #MeToo movement arrived. Formally started in 2006 by civil rights activist Tarana Burke, #MeToo went viral in 2017 when news reports started coming out that the highly influential movie producer Harvey Weinstein had sexually harassed and abused numerous women over decades. This news seemed to open the floodgates for a new and intense level of attention to the issue of sexual harassment. Women were suddenly increasingly empowered to use their voices, tell their stories, engage with the legal system, and demand change. This critical amplifying of the woman's voice has significantly affected workplace and recreational environments. It also seemed to have led to many men feeling more comfortable giving voice to their own cases of being sexually harassed or assaulted. This was a departure from men's tendency to be disconnected from their emotional lives, the way a traditional patriarchal system says they should be. On an increasingly grand scale, voices of victimization were boldly asserting their needs. This was a prime endeavor of Carol's and it was being more fully realized than ever before.

TRY THIS

What is Your School Like?

Do you know what your school's (or past schools') policies are? Do they have a restorative discipline policy? Do they have a focus on social-emotional topics as well as academic ones? Do you know who your school counselor is, where their office is, and when they're available? What's your school's approach towards gender identity? Try to find out, if you don't know. And then think about whether the school's policies are supporting students in the best way possible. If they're not—what can you do about it?

EPILOGUE

In 2019, Carol participated in a book event at the famous Strand bookstore in New York City for *Why Does Patriarchy Persist?* Toward the end of the evening, a teenage girl asked Carol what advice she would give to young girls who wanted to resist but didn't want to be labeled "nasty or angry women." Carol replied simply, "Well, you are going to be labeled. The question is, 'What is your response?'" This has remained an important question that demands a good answer.

In 2023, Carol's latest book, *In a Human Voice*, was published, 40 years after *In a Different Voice* altered the landscape of psychology forever. In this new book, Carol seeks to unify her ideas over the decades. It builds on the themes of voice, activism, resistance, and liberation, reinforcing their relevance in the 21st century and beyond, while offering readers a compass in navigating toward a more caring, ethical, and democratic society for everyone.

Earlier in 2023, when Sarah Polley, the director of the film *Women Talking*, won the Academy Award for Best Adapted Screenplay, she emphasized the need for a responsive voice. The movie is about a group of victimized women living in a remote Mennonite community who empower themselves to change their fate. During her acceptance speech, Polley referenced the film's final line, spoken by a young woman to her new baby: "Your story will be different from ours." Thanks to Carol Gilligan, the story of future generations may very well be a far different one from our own.

TIMELINE

1837
1848
1859
1920
1922

1837: Oberlin College is the first U.S. university to go co-educational

1920: The Nineteenth Amendment to the U.S. Constitution is passed, giving White women the right to vote. Widely considered the end of First-Wave Feminism

1848: Elizabeth Cady Stanton and other leaders host The Seneca Falls Women's Rights Convention, kicking off the beginning of First-Wave Feminism

1922: Rebecca Felton of Georgia is the first woman to serve on the U.S. Senate

1859: Charles Darwin publishes *On the Origin of Species*

1936 / **1939** / **1958** / **1960s** ⤳

1936: Carol is born to parents William Friedman and Mabel Caminez

1939: Carol and her mother attend the Clara Thompson's institute at Vassar College

1960s: Second-Wave Feminism, focusing on sexuality, reproductive rights, and the broader patriarchal tendencies of society, begins, lasting into the 1990s

1958: Carol graduates summa cum laude from Swarthmore College with a BA in English Literature

1958: Kohlberg's Stages of Moral Development is published

TIMELINE

1961

1963

1964

1963: Dr. Martin Luther King Jr. and other Civil Rights leaders lead the March on Washington

1961: Carol graduates from Radcliffe College with a Master's degree in Clinical Psychology

1961: Carol marries James Gilligan

1964: Carol graduates from Harvard University with a PhD in social psychology

1964: The Civil Rights Act is passed, outlawing discrimination on the basis of race, color, religion, sex, and national origin, and ending legal segregation

1965

March 7-21, 1965: Civil Rights leaders lead a March from Selma to Montgomery, Alabama, to protest voting restrictions

August 6, 1965: The Voting Rights Act is passed, which prohibits racial discrimination in voting, and gives people of color the right to vote

1965: First active U.S. ground troops enter the Vietnam War, and remain a presence there until 1973

TIMELINE

1972 / 1973 / 1982 / 1983

1972: Title IX is passed, prohibiting sex-based discrimination in any educational setting that receives funding from the government

1982: *In a Different Voice* is published by Harvard University Press

1983: Columbia University begins accepting women students to its main campus, the last Ivy League university to do so

1973: Supreme Court rules on Roe v. Wade, ruling that the Constitution of the United States protected the right of an individual to an abortion

1984: Carol named *Ms.* magazine's woman of the year

1984: Geraldine Ferraro becomes first woman to be a U.S. vice presidential nominee

1991: Anita Hill testifies during Clarence Thomas's Supreme Court confirmation hearing about alleged sexual harassment. Often considered the launching point of Third-Wave Feminism, which has a greater focus on intersectionality and bodily autonomy

TIMELINE

1993

1996

1997

1993: First "Take Our Daughters to Work Day"

1996: Carol named one of Time magazine's 25 Most Influential People

1993: Gender Equity in Education Act passed

1997: Carol helps establish, and becomes the first head of, the Gender Studies Department at Harvard University's Graduate School of Education

1998 / **2017** / **2022**

1998: Carol receives $250,000 Heinz Award in recognition of her work deepening our understanding of the human condition

2017: #MeToo movement starts

2022: The Supreme Court overturns the previous decision on Roe v. Wade, eliminating federal protections on abortion rights

CAN YOU HEAR ME NOW? #MeToo WE WERE NEVER SILENT. WE WERE SILENCED. AND IGNORED

GLOSSARY

19th Amendment: amendment to the U.S. Constitution, passed in 1920, that made it so people could not be denied the right to vote based on their sex, therefore granting women the right to vote.

Biological Sex: an assignment usually given at birth predicated on observation of genitalia and/or determination of chromosomes and anatomical structures of the body at birth. "Male," "female," and "intersex" are terms for biological sex.

Control Group: a group in a study whose members receive either no intervention at all or some established intervention, in order to compare results with the experimental group.

Democracy: a form of government in which the people either participate in the political process themselves or elect others to do so on their behalf (representative democracy) and in which decisions are made by majority vote.

Diversity, Equity, and Inclusion (DEI) Frameworks: groups and policies within organizations (especially workplaces) that actively seek to make sure there is equal representation and opportunities for all groups of people.

Double-Blind Study: a study in which neither the researchers nor the participants know which groups are the control group and which are the experimental group, in order to prevent bias.

Ethic of Care: in contrast to the Ethic of Justice, Carol Gilligan's theory that moral choices are often based on interpersonal relationships and how choices will affect each other, as much as black and white concepts of right or wrong.

Ethic of Justice: a term used by Carol Gilligan to describe the type of "right or wrong" reasoning and decision-making shown in Lawrence's Kohlberg's model of the stages of moral development, which focused mainly on men.

Experimental Group: a group of participants in a research study who are exposed to the independent variable.

First-wave Feminism: a largely political movement in the 19th century, focused (in the United States) on women's suffrage and political and economic opportunities, especially with women's right to vote.

Gender: a social construct and social identity based on the attitudes, feelings, and behaviors that a given culture associates with a person's biological sex. "Man," "woman," "boy," "girl," etc. are expressions of gender.

The Listening Guide Method: a method of psychological analysis created by Carol Gilligan that draws on voice, resonance, and relationship as ports of entry into the human psyche.

LSD: lysergic acid diethylamide, also known as "acid," a highly potent hallucinogen.

MeToo Movement: a social movement meant to bring awareness to sexual abuse and harassment. The phrase was originally started in 2006 by activist Tarana Burke but popularized in 2017 as a hashtag, with which women all over the world shared their own experiences.

Patriarchy: a society in which descent and inheritance is traced through the male only; or, more loosely, a family, group, or society in which men are dominant.

Restorative Justice: an approach to criminal justice in which emphasis is placed on rehabilitation of offenders and repairing the harm done to victims rather than on punishment.

Roe v. Wade: a Supreme Court Decision in 1973 in which it was decided that the right to have an abortion was protected in the United States. This decision was overturned in 2022.

Second-wave Feminism: a movement from the early 1960s through the early 1990s that focused on more wide-ranging issues of gender equality, such as familial and gender roles, reproductive rights, equal pay, and more.

Social-Emotional Learning: the idea that learning to recognize, process, and cope with emotions and social interactions is an important part of a child's development and education.

Socioeconomic Status: the income, educational attainment, occupational prestige, and subjective perceptions of social status and social class of a person or group.

The Still-Face Experiment: an experiment done by Dr. Ed Tronick in 1970 that showed that infants reacted negatively to an expressionless face on their caregivers.

Take Our Daughters to Work Day: an event originally created by Ms. Foundation for Women president, Marie C. Wilson, treasurer, Darren Ball, and founder, Gloria Steinem in 1992 with the aim of giving girls a glimpse into the working world and encouraging them to pursue whatever career they were interested in, despite gender stereotypes. It now includes boys as well, and is called Take Our Daughters and Sons to Work Day or Take Your Child to Work Day.

Title IX: a law passed as part of the Education Amendments of 1972 in the United States, which prohibits sex-based discrimination in any education program or activity that receives federal funding (therefore including most schools).

FURTHER READING

American Psychological Association Principles of Social-Emotional Learning
apa.org/ed/schools/teaching-learning/top-twenty/
principles/social-emotional-learning

Committee for Children
cfchildren.org

Ethical and Moral Dilemmas for Classroom Discussion
goodcharacter.com/the-daily-dilemma

In a Different Voice: Psychology Theory and Women's Development
by Carol Gilligan, published by Harvard University Press.

In a Human Voice
by Carol Gilligan, published by Polity.

National Child Traumatic Stress Network
nctsn.org

Project for the Advancement of Our Common Humanity (PACH)
pach.org

Take Our Daughters and Sons to Work Foundation
daughtersandsonstowork.org

The Good Project
thegoodproject.org

University of San Diego Center for Restorative Justice
sandiego.edu/soles/centers-and-institutes/restorative-justice

Why Does Patriarchy Persist?
by Carol Gilligan and Naomi Snider, published by Polity.

BIBLIOGRAPHY

American Psychological Association. (n.d.). *Dictionary of psychology.* https://dictionary.apa.org/

Alvarez, B. (2022, March 30). What educators can do to help dismantle the school-to-prison pipeline. *NEA Today.* Retrieved from: https://www.nea.org/nea-today/all-news-articles/what-educators-can-do-help-dismantle-school-prison-pipeline

Brown, L. M. & Gilligan, C. (1992). *Meeting at the crossroads.* Cambridge, MA: Harvard University Press.

Centers for Disease Control and Prevention. (2023, February 13). *U.S. Teen girls experiencing increased sadness and violence.* Retrieved from: https://www.cdc.gov/media/releases/2023/p0213-yrbs.html

Gewertz, K. (2001, March 8). Fonda donates $12.5M to GSE. *Harvard Gazette.* Retrieved from: https://news.harvard.edu/gazette/story/2001/03/fonda-donates-12-5m-to-gse/

Gilligan, C. (1982). *In a different voice: Psychological theory and women's development.* Harvard University Press.

Gilligan, C. (1994). Getting civilized. *Fordham Law Review, 63*(1). Retrieved from: https://ir.lawnet.fordham.edu/cgi/viewcontent.cgi?httpsredir=1&article=3124&context=flr

Gilligan, C. (2002). *The birth of pleasure: A new map of love.* Knopf Doubleday.

Gilligan, C. (2009, September 15). *Interview by L. Granek* [Video Recording]. Psychology's Feminist Voices and Oral History and Online Archive Project. Retrieved from: https://feministvoices.com/files/profiles/pdf/Carol-Gilligan-Oral-History.pdf

Gilligan, C. (2023). *In a human voice*. Polity.

Gilligan, C., & Eddy, J. (2021). The listening guide: Replacing judgment with curiosity. *Qualitative Psychology, 8*(2), 141–151. https://doi.org/10.1037/qup0000213

Gilligan, C. & Snider, N. (2018). *Why does patriarchy persist?* Polity.

Gilligan, C., Spencer, R., Weinberg, M. K., & Bertsch, T. (2003). On the Listening Guide: A voice-centered relational method. In P. M. Camic, J. E. Rhodes, & L. Yardley (Eds.), *Qualitative research in psychology: Expanding perspectives in methodology and design* (pp. 157–172). American Psychological Association. https://doi.org/10.1037/10595-009

Goldberg, M. (2000). Restoring lost voices: An interview with Carol Gilligan. *The Phi Delta Kappan, 81*(9) 701–702, 704. https://www.proquest.com/scholarly-journals/restoring-lost-voices-interview-with-carol/docview/218474329/se-2

Green, P. (2019, March 18). Carefully smash the patriarchy. *The New York Times*. Retrieved from: https://www.nytimes.com/2019/03/18/style/carol-gilligan.html

Hoff Sommers, C. (2000, May). The war against boys. *The Atlantic*. Retrieved from: https://www.theatlantic.com/magazine/archive/2000/05/the-war-against-boys/304659/

Josselson, R. (2023). Developing a different voice: The life and work of Carol Gilligan. *Journal of Personality, 91*(1). https://doi.org/10.1111/jopy.12763

National Child Traumatic Stress Network. (2017). *Creating, supporting, and sustaining trauma-informed schools: A system framework*. Retrieved from: https://www.samhsa.gov/sites/default/files/programs_campaigns/childrens_mental_health/nctsi-creating-supporting-sustaining-trauma-informed-schools-a-systems-framework.pdf

Ohlheiser, A. (2017, October 19). The woman behind 'Me Too' knew the power of the phrase when she created it – 10 years ago. *The Washington Post.* Retrieved from: https://www.washingtonpost.com/news/the-intersect/wp/2017/10/19/the-woman-behind-me-too-knew-the-power-of-the-phrase-when-she-created-it-10-years-ago/

Viadero, D. (1998). Their own voices. *Education Week.* Retrieved from: https://www.edweek.org/education/their-own-voices/1998/05

Waldinger, R. & Schulz, M. (2023, January 19). What the longest study on human happiness found is the key to a good life. *The Atlantic.* Retrieved from: https://www.theatlantic.com/ideas/archive/2023/01/harvard-happiness-study-relationships/672753/

Waxman, O. B. (2017, April 26). The inside story of why Take Your Daughter To Work Day exists. *Time Magazine.* Retrieved from: https://time.com/4753128/take-your-our-daughters-to-work-day-history/

Wilkinson, F. (2020, March 5). Elizabeth Warren's graceful surrender. *Bloomberg.* Retrieved from: https://www.bloomberg.com/view/articles/2020-03-05/warren-s-withdrawal-shows-how-far-women-have-come-and-must-yet-go

PHOTO CREDITS

Page 118: Civil Rights March on Washington, D.C. (Dr. Martin Luther King, Jr. and Mathew Ahmann in a crowd.), Rowland Scherman, Public domain, via Wikimedia Commons

Page 118: Lyndon Johnson signing Civil Rights Act, July 2, 1964, Cecil Stoughton, White House Press Office (WHPO), Public domain, via Wikimedia Commons

Page 119: Lyndon Johnson and Martin Luther King, Jr., Voting Rights Act, Yoichi Okamoto, Public domain, via Wikimedia Commons

Page 119: Abernathy Children Lead The SELMA TO MONTGOMERY MARCH, Mrs. Donza Leigh abernathy, CC BY-SA creativecommons.org licenses by-sa 4.0, via Wikimedia Commons

Page 119: Vietnam Veterans Memorial Statue 2023, Mojnsen, CC BY-SA 4.0 creativecommons.org licenses by-sa 4.0, via Wikimedia Commons.

Page 120: Senator Birch Bayh addresses a group of students, Birch Bayh Senate Office, Public domain, via Wikimedia Commons

Page 120: Burger Court in 1973, US Government, Public domain, via Wikimedia Commons

Page 121: Geraldine Ferraro congressional portrait, U.S. House of Representatives, Public domain, via Wikimedia Commons

Page 121: Anita Hill testifying in front of the Senate Judiciary Committee, R. Michael Jenkins, Public domain, via Wikimedia Commons

Page 123: Can You Hear Me Now-MeToo, Alec Perkins from Hoboken, USA, CC BY 2.0 creativecommons.org licenses by 2.0, via Wikimedia Commons

Page 134: Bill Cole and Carol Gilligan by James Gilligan

Carol Gilligan and Bill Cole

Bill Cole is a school psychologist based in New Jersey. He is also an adjunct professor of developmental psychology at Fairleigh Dickinson University, in which he teaches Carol Gilligan's Ethic of Care model. He has been a guest columnist for the Newark Star-Ledger, writing numerous articles on public education, child development, and politics. He is also an award-winning fiction writer, whose work has appeared in *Highlights for Children Magazine*.

Sarah Green graduated from RISD in 2014 with a BFA in Illustration and began her career in children's books in 2015, with over a dozen solo-illustrated picture books, as well as several covers and middle grade books. She has also illustrated a line of stationary for Trader Joes, had a regular role illustrating a column in the *New York Times*, and has worked with a range of editorial clients, including Sephora, The British Library, and Hearst Corporation. Sarah received her MFA from Emily Carr University of Art + Design in 2021, and currently teaches in the Illustration Department there alongside working as a full time illustrator. Sarah is from the San Francisco Bay Area and lives in Vancouver, Canada. Visit sarahgreenillustration.com, @s_green_bean on X, and @sarahgreenstudio on Instagram.

Magination Press is the children's book imprint of the American Psychological Association. APA works to advance psychology as a science and profession and as a means of promoting health and human welfare. Magination Press books reach young readers and their parents and caregivers to make navigating life's challenges a little easier. It's the combined power of psychology and literature that makes a Magination Press book special. Visit maginationpress.org and @MaginationPress on Facebook, X, Instagram, and Pinterest.